BLACK WOMEN WHO DARED

NAOMI M. MOYER

Second Story Press
www.secondstorypress.ca

CONTENTS

WE OFTEN DARE because we have to. So many Black women were feminists before the word *feminist* was even in our vocabularies. We are radical in every way: radical healers, community organizers, entrepreneurs, educators, and mothers. We are innovative to our very core. *Black Women Who Dared* shares ten biographies of women and groups who were committed to uplifting their communities in every magical and resourceful way imaginable. Their stories are unique because they all take place in North America and involve largely uncelebrated women who created opportunities for themselves and those they cared about. When thinking of the Great Migration from the American South, we realize it didn't end in Los Angeles, Chicago, or New York City. It carried on through to Vancouver, Toronto, and Montreal and often times back south again. Growing up in Northern British Columbia, I never imagined the rich histories involving Black people here in Canada. What a treat and matter of pride it would have been to learn about Black women in Canadian history at my public school. In this lovingly written and illustrated book, you can connect with women such as Rosa Pryor—Vancouver's first Black woman business owner—and a collective of international nurses who provided essential health care to Black communities. Curl up with your loved ones, your little ones, or even yourself and soak up the vibrant colors and lives these fabulous women chose to live.

THE COLOURED WOMEN'S CLUB was founded over a century ago in 1902 in Montreal, Quebec. Although many of the women who founded the club were married with busy families, they were determined to have a voice and a place where they could organize and socialize and serve their community. They were following the example of the National Association of Colored Women's Clubs (NACWC), founded in the 1890s in Washington, DC, by Harriet Tubman and others. Because Black women were excluded by other clubs, the best thing to do was establish a club of their very own. As a result, The Coloured Women's Club, under the guidance of Anne Greenup, focused on supporting Black communities in Montreal, specifically the area known today as Little Burgundy.

During the next hundred years, the club grew to be a large and reliable resource for Black families. Basic needs that were not being met locally were served through the club, such as temporary shelters, soup kitchens, and food and winter clothing drives. Initially, the club was a social outlet for its members, but with wars and flu epidemics and the overall oppression affecting Black people, it quickly became an important aid to people in need. From assisting sick or injured war veterans, to counseling single mothers, many members volunteered in hospitals and homes across Montreal.

The women were so innovative that their work influenced many professionals in what is known today as social work. From operating a small Black history library, to arranging burial services for those who couldn't afford them, to providing childcare, the Coloured Women's Club did it all. To this day, the club is still active with twelve members who meet in one another's homes. The focus now is mainly on organizing scholarships for Black youth.

JACKIE SHANE is a musical legend who was well before her time. She was born in Nashville, Tennessee in 1940. From an early age, she didn't identify as a boy, the gender that was assigned to her at birth. It was difficult for a Black person living in the South at that time, but being Black and transgender was doubly difficult and very dangerous. Yet, with the loving support of her family, Jackie was able to thrive and embrace her true self. She became a professional drummer and performed as a dancer and singer with a traveling carnival. By 1959, she had made her way to Canada.

In Montreal, Jackie was invited to sing with Frank Motley and his Motley Crew band. Before long, Jackie became the band's lead vocalist. By 1962, she had a song on the Top 10 charts called "Any Other Way" and was living in Toronto. This single remained on Toronto's CHUM Chart for twenty weeks straight. For over a decade, Jackie performed regularly in Canada and the United States. Jackie's gender confused many people who called her a "cross dresser" and made fun of her. With grace, Jackie laughed in the face of discrimination and continued to make a living doing what she loved.

Jackie was as much a pioneer as she was a performer and musician because she tackled taboo subjects such as gender identity, sexuality, and racism decades before they were discussed openly. She set the stage for many people to break gender barriers. After years of mistreatment, Jackie bravely left the Motley Crew band and moved back to the States for the last time. She turned down many career opportunities and advancements in order to care for her elderly mother. She has since moved back to her hometown of Nashville and is now in her late seventies.

Over a century old, **SYLVIA ESTES STARK** lived to be one hundred and six. She was born in 1839, in Clay County, Missouri when slavery was still legal and she was enslaved with the rest of her family. As soon as she was able, Sylvia had to work. During her childhood she secretly taught herself to read and write. She also developed two personalities in order to survive. She used one around white people and the other—her real self—around her family.

Sylvia's father was so determined to free his family that he moved to California where slavery was illegal and he could earn money working. Two years later he returned with his savings to buy his family's freedom. The family, reunited and free, went with him to California. Sylvia was twelve at the time. Four years later, at age sixteen, she married Louis Stark. Although slavery was prohibited in California, there were many laws in place to protect white people and enable racism and oppression. The Fugitive Slave Act made it even more dangerous for Black Californians to live comfortably.

In 1858, the Governor of British Columbia, Sir James Douglas, invited concerned Black families to Vancouver Island. He needed more people in his newly formed colony and he promised them freedom and fair treatment. The whole Stark family journeyed to Canada by boat. Sylvia and Louis eventually moved to Salt Spring Island and began living off the land. But Louis' work left Sylvia and their children alone for weeks at a time. As a result, Sylvia developed many skills, from fending off wild animals to learning the Chinook Wawa trade language. She dedicated her life to serving her family and community as a farmer, a nurse, and a midwife. She had seven children and for the last sixty years of her life she lived with her eldest son, Willis. Together, they grew vegetables and raised pigs, goats, cows, and chickens. Sylvia outlived Willis, who died at age eighty-five, by one year. Her descendants live throughout Canada and the United States.

When fifteen Black women met informally over tea to talk about what it was like to be Black women living in Windsor, Ontario, they simply wanted to see better support for Black people and improvement within themselves. What started off being called The Mother's Club in 1934, blossomed into **THE HOUR-A-DAY STUDY CLUB** in 1935. Members decided to dedicate sixty minutes a day to studying a variety of subjects to improve their parenting skills and to broaden their knowledge outside of motherhood. This was during a time when restaurants refused to serve Black people and schools were segregated. It was also during the Great Depression, which was hard for many, but especially hard for Black people.

The club members studied, read, and advocated for child literacy. They encouraged children not only to stay in school but also to excel in school. There was also a focus on teaching children to work together to solve larger issues that affected their community as a whole. What was once a club focused on education, became more political and created an opportunity for Black women to become activists. Combating racism and sexism were just as important as studying Black history. Club members advocated for young Black women to be accepted into nursing programs by writing the Ministry of Health. They also raised funds for a local man who experienced police brutality and needed legal support. The Hour-a-Day Study Club changed along with the current issues that affected Black communities. Members became visible role models. Today, the club is still active and provides scholarships for Black students.

ROSA PRYOR, also known as Mama Pryor, was the first Black woman to own a business in Vancouver. She was born in 1887 in the United States and moved to Vancouver, British Columbia in 1917, hoping for a better future. Without a nickel to her name, she opened up her very own restaurant in 1919, just two years after coming to Canada. Rosa had convinced a complete stranger to lend her twenty dollars so she could buy a business license. Her restaurant was called Chicken Inn and was famous for its fried chicken. Chicken Inn was the first establishment in Vancouver to introduce Southern soul food.

Rosa literally opened up her home to her customers by running the restaurant from her small living room. She managed to fit in six tables, a jukebox, a piano, and to serve about one hundred hungry people on busy nights. Her restaurant was not only known for its food, but also for the pianists and gospel singers who performed there. Chicken Inn was a home away from home; a place to dance, enjoy live music, eat home cooking, and socialize. It also provided jobs to many Black women who lived in Rosa's neighborhood known as Hogan's Alley. Hogan's Alley was the first Black neighborhood in Vancouver. It was nestled within Chinatown, a direct supplier of chicken for the restaurant. In short order, Rosa was able to pay back the twenty dollars and she never had to borrow money again. Chicken Inn was open for roughly thirty years.

SHERONA HALL was born in Kingston, Jamaica in 1948 and became dedicated to justice and equality at a young age. She campaigned for a local political party and was a founding member of its youth organization before she was old enough to vote. When Sherona's family moved to Canada, she hit the ground running as an activist. One of the first issues she tackled from her home base in Toronto, was unfit working conditions for newcomers from the Caribbean. Later, she would found the Committee Against the Deportation of Immigrant Women to help those who were facing unfair deportations.

For forty years, Sherona worked tirelessly to help her community. Whatever problems Black people faced, Sherona was ready to listen, organize, and advocate. She addressed issues of labor, gender, youth, health, education, housing, police violence, and immigration. Sherona understood that all injustices needed to be challenged because they were all connected to uplifting Black people. Sherona's community extended from Canada, to the Caribbean, to Africa, and beyond. Nothing was too big or too small for her to take on. If there was a problem, it mattered. But fighting injustice was not Sherona's only focus. Celebrating African history and culture, especially music, was just as important to her.

Whether it was a child in school, a peer, an activist, an elder, or a leader, Sherona was a friend who treated everyone with equal respect. She worked so hard helping others that she sometimes forgot to take care of herself. Communities far and wide lost their friend Sherona in 1996, but her energy, kinship, and dedication are remembered by many to this day.

THE BLACK CROSS NURSES is an international organization that was created by Black women in 1920. It was formed for two major reasons: Black people did not have equal access to health care and Black women were rarely admitted into nursing programs because of their race. The organization's purpose was not only to provide essential health care in communities, but also to provide training and opportunities for Black women.

This organization was founded by Henrietta Vinton Davis in Philadelphia, Pennsylvania, but by 1927 it had expanded into Central America, the Caribbean, and Canada. In Canada, branches formed in Ontario, Nova Scotia, Quebec, and British Columbia mostly because Black women hadn't been allowed to participate in aiding soldiers during World War I. Some women were nurses with formal medical training and some were midwives, but most members had only basic training in first aid.

Determined, but with very basic training, these women provided essential health care services within Black communities all across the Americas. Their services were holistic and adapted to the needs of the people. This organization influenced health policies, helped wounded soldiers, assisted those affected by natural disasters, provided childcare, promoted literacy and proper nutrition, and even distributed clothing and food where there was a need. Although most chapters disappeared over time, there are still active members throughout the United States.

MARY MILES BIBB was born in 1820 when most Black people in the U.S. were still enslaved. But Mary was fortunate to have been born within a free Black Quaker family from Rhode Island. As a result, she was allowed to study and graduate, becoming one of the first Black women teachers in the United States. Mary was happy, but would have been happier knowing that all Black people could have the same opportunities. Mary was not only a teacher, but also an abolitionist—someone who wanted to get rid of slavery. It was while doing anti-slavery work that she met, and later married, Henry Bibb.

In 1850, the Fugitive Slave Act was passed in the U.S. This act gave slaveholders more power to search for and recapture those runaways who had fled to the Northern U.S. Since Henry was one of those who escaped, he and Mary decided it would be safer to move to Canada West (now Ontario). They settled in Sandwich, Ontario where Mary ran a school for Black children out of their home since many schools were segregated at that time.

Eventually the couple moved to Windsor, Ontario where Mary continued to help improve lives in Black communities. There was much to be done. Mary and Henry opened up their home to provide shelter for many families who had arrived as refugees via the Underground Railroad—a network of safe houses where runaways, in a bid to escape enslavement, could hide and rest as they traveled on foot from the Southern States to the North hoping to live in freedom. Together, they assisted formerly enslaved folks to settle in Canada with land and a place to live. Mary, Henry, and a few others also began publishing a newspaper called the *Voice of the Fugitive*. The newspaper did just what its name suggested. It gave a voice to Black people and their quest for freedom. The *Voice of the Fugitive* was the first Black-owned newspaper in Canada.

Tragedy struck on Emancipation Day in August of 1854 when Mary's husband, Henry, passed away. She continued to teach and worked running a store for six years. Eventually, Mary moved back to the States to continue teaching until she passed away in 1877.

Slavery is a part of North America's past and **CHLOE COOLEY**, a young enslaved woman, made history in Upper Canada in 1793. Chloe kept her self-respect by reclaiming her own freedom through bold acts such as: refusing to work, leaving her workplace without permission, and "borrowing" items that didn't belong to her. Such behavior was very brave because in those days, if enslaved people did anything without their master's permission, they risked harsh punishment—sometimes even death.

Word had been spreading that the laws of Upper Canada might soon change to make slave-owning illegal. Those who had invested in the slave trade were becoming nervous. If slavery were abolished, their investments would become worthless. Many owners started selling off their "property" across the border in the United States, where slavery was still legal. Chloe's master intended to do the same with her, and in fact he did, but not without a great deal of difficulty. He and another man beat her, tied her up, and forced her onto a boat. This boat would take her across the Niagara River into the United States, where her chances of ever being free again were very slim.

With nothing to lose, Chloe decided to show her master—and everyone else—that what they were doing was wrong. She fought with every muscle, screamed with all her voice, and made such a scene that her master was charged and taken to court. Although Chloe didn't win her fight to stay in Canada, her courage and strength set the stage for The Act to Limit Slavery and the Slavery Abolition Act. Once those acts passed, the Underground Railroad was firmly established. An estimated 100,000 people made it to safety between 1800 and 1865 due in no small part to Chloe Cooley's brave stand for freedom. She will always be remembered and admired.

BLOCKORAMA, better known as Blocko, was created to make a space for the Black LGBTTI2QQ community within Toronto's Pride Parade. Blocko is an all-day celebration of Blackness of all genders and sexualities; a celebration of love, including self-love. One of the founding members is a feminist, educator, and activist named Jamea Zuberi. The first party was held in a parking lot in 1998. Imagine an empty, gray parking lot transformed into a vibrant space filled with music, family, and friends performing, dancing, and socializing. What a beautiful thing!

After many years of not feeling included or represented by Pride, Jamea was determined to make room for her community, while helping Pride to be more inclusive. Jamea contacted Angela Robertson, Camille Orridge, and others to share ideas. Their first meeting was in Jamea's living room. During these meetings the name Blackness Yes was created for the organizing committee. After many meetings, phone calls, letters, and fundraisers the first Blocko party took place. It was essentially a block party, very much inspired by Jamea's childhood street-party memories.

Although Pride funds Blocko, it remains underfunded, and over the years there have been many struggles to keep a solid venue within Pride. Like Pride, Blocko is not just about partying. It's more about taking up space within spaces that don't include you. It is a powerful way to show that being queer, being trans, and being Black matters. It also commemorates the many pioneers of Pride who were Black. For twenty years now, Blocko has shape-shifted and has expanded into Caribana as Blockobana, a huge family-friendly picnic. Both parties host local and international artists and attract thousands of people every year.

For my daughter, Aluwa Simmone.
–NMM–

Library and Archives Canada Cataloguing in Publication

Moyer, Naomi M., 1977-, author
Black women who dared / Naomi M. Moyer.

ISBN 978-1-77260-071-1 (hardcover)

1. Women, Black--Canada--Biography--Juvenile literature.
2. Black Canadian women--Biography--Juvenile literature. 3. Women,
Black--Canada--History--Juvenile literature. 4. Black Canadian
women--History--Juvenile literature. 5. Canada--Biography--Juvenile
literature. I. Title.

FC106.B6M69 2018   j305.48'896071   C2018-901633-7

Second Story Press gratefully acknowledges the support
of the Ontario Arts Council and the Canada Council for the Arts for
our publishing program. We acknowledge the financial support of the
Government of Canada through the Canada Book Fund.

Second Story Press would also like to thank Talin Vartanian for
introducing us to Naomi Moyer's art.

Published by
Second Story Press
20 Maud Street, Suite 401
Toronto, Ontario, Canada
M5V 2M5
www.secondstorypress.ca